ELEPHANTS NEVER FORGET!

Make Me Laugh!

ELEPHANTS NEVER FORGET!

a book of elephant jokes

by Diane L. Burns / pictures by Joan Hanson

Lerner Publications Company · Minneapolis

*To Breneman and Korry for their inspiration and for
being faithful "family" with laughter and hugs. I love
you both.*

This book is available in two editions:
Library binding by Lerner Publications Company
Soft cover by First Avenue Editions
241 First Avenue North
Minneapolis, Minnesota 55401

Copyright © 1987 by Lerner Publications Company

Library of Congress Cataloging-in-Publication Data

Burns, Diane L.
  Elephants never forget!

  (Make me laugh!)
  Summary: A collection of elephant jokes, including
"What's the hardest thing for a stampeding elephant
to catch? Her breath."
  1. Elephants—Juvenile humor. 2. Wit and humor,
Juvenile. 3. Riddles, Juvenile. [1. Elephants—Wit
and humor. 2. Jokes. 3. Riddles] I. Hanson, Joan,
ill. II. Title. III. Series.
PN6231.E5B8   1987   818′.5402   86-18579
ISBN 0-8225-0992-X (lib. bdg.)
ISBN 0-8225-9518-4 (pbk.)

Manufactured in the United States of America

1 2 3 4 5 6 7 8 9 10 96 95 94 93 92 91 90 89 88 87

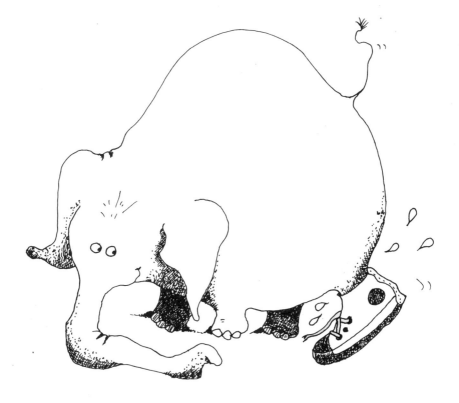

Q: What goes clomp, clomp, clomp, swish, clomp, clomp, clomp, swish?

A: An elephant with one wet tennis shoe.

Q: Why did the elephant change her socks on the golf course?

A: She got a hole in one.

Q: How did the cowboy elephant burn himself?

A: Trying to make himself at home on the range.

Q: Why did the elephant wear green tennis shoes?

A: Because his blue ones were wet.

Q: Why did the elephant wear sunglasses?
A: She didn't want to be noticed.

Q: Why was the elephant's face blue?
A: His tennis shoes were tied too tight.

Q: Why don't elephants do well in karate class?
A: Even when their belts aren't too tight, they can't kick very high.

Q: What's the hardest thing for a stampeding elephant to catch?
A: Her breath.

Q: Do elephant tourists like to go swimming?

A: Yes, when they remember to pack their trunks.

Q: How does an elephant make a strawberry shake?

A: She takes it to a scary movie.

Q: Why did the elephant take a raisin to the movies?

A: He couldn't find a date.

Q: What does an elephant use during a sad movie?

A: JUMBO-sized tissues.

Q: What kind of elephant can you find in a box of popcorn?

A: A very small one.

Q: Why did the elephant eat bullets?
A: She wanted to grow bangs.

Q: What's an elephant's favorite Christmas carol?
A: "Jungle Bells."

Q: What does an elephant have that no other animal has?
A: Baby elephants.

Q: When will an elephant use your shower?
A: After a hot day of stampeding.

Q: What do you call the first elephant in the bathtub?

A: The ringleader.

Q: Why aren't there any elephants in outer space?

A: Because they take up too much *inner* space.

Q: Where do baby elephants sleep?

A: In trunk-beds.

Q: When should you put an elephant in your sister's bed?

A: When you can't find a frog.

Q: What's worse than having an elephant in bed with you?

A: *Two* elephants.

Q: What is as big as an elephant but weighs absolutely nothing?

A: An elephant's shadow.

Q: What has four legs, a trunk, and a tail and sees just as well from either end?

A: An elephant with his eyes shut.

Q: What's gray and has four legs and a trunk?

A: A mouse on vacation.

Q: What's gray, has big ears and four legs, and weighs five pounds?

A: A *very* skinny elephant.

Q: Can an elephant jump higher than a house?

A: Yes, houses can't jump at all.

Q: Where do baby elephants come from?

A: *Huge* storks.

Q: What looks just like an elephant?

A: Another elephant.

Q: What do you do with a blue elephant?

A: Cheer her up.

Q: How does an elephant make a bedroll?

A: He pushes it downhill.

Q: Why did the elephant eat under the lamppost?

A: She wanted a light lunch.

Q: What happened to the elephant that swallowed his spoon?

A: He couldn't stir.

Q: Why wouldn't the ant rent his attic to an elephant?

A: He was afraid the elephant would put his foot down.

Q: What happened when the elephant tried to fix her neighbor's roof?

A: She brought down the house.

Q: Why did the elephant cross the road?
A: To prove she wasn't a chicken.

Q: How can you tell if there's an elephant in your kitchen?
A: Look for footprints in the peanut butter.

Q: How can you tell if your cook is an elephant?
A: He'll flatten the oatmeal cookies with his feet.

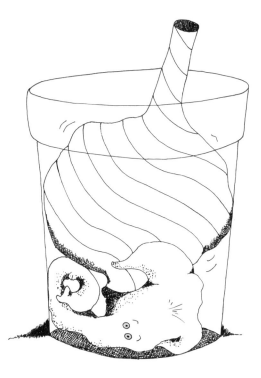

Q: How can you tell if there's an elephant in your milkshake?

A: It's really hard to suck anything up the straw.

Q: In what Olympic event do elephants always take first place?

A: Herd-les.

Q: What happened to the elephant who slid into third base?

A: Nothing much happened to the elephant, but it was rough on the base.

Q: How do elephant basketball teams score points?

A: They slam-trunk the ball.

Q: What time is it when an elephant jumps rope?

A: Time to call for street repairs.

Q: What do you get when you cross an elephant with peanut butter?

A: An elephant that sticks to the roof of your mouth.

Q: How can you tell if there's an elephant on your key chain?

A: It won't fit in your pocket.

Q: How can you tell if there's an elephant hiding in your piano?

A: He'll sing along while you practice.

Q: How can you find the elephants in a chorus line?

A: Just look for their dimpled knees.

Q: How can you tell if an elephant is reading over your shoulder?

A: You can smell the peanuts on his breath.

Q: What must a circus trainer know before she can teach tricks to an elephant?

A: More than the elephant.

Q: What do you call an elephant with a diploma?

A: Smart.

Q: How is an owl like an elephant?
A: Neither one can ride a bicycle.

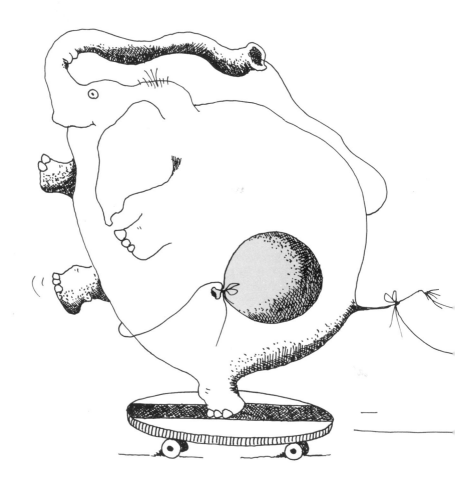

ABOUT THE AUTHOR

DIANE L. BURNS, her husband, and their two sons spend their summers "on top of the world" as firetower lookouts in Idaho's River of No Return Wilderness. During the rest of the year, Diane and her family live on a maple sugar farm in Rhinelander, Wisconsin. A natural resources graduate of UW-Stevens Point and former sixth grade teacher, Diane spends her free time cheering (loudly) at her sons' athletic games and writing stories for children. She also enjoys meeting people and sharing food and laughter with friends.

ABOUT THE ARTIST

JOAN HANSON lives with her husband and two sons in Afton, Minnesota. Her distinctive, deliberately whimsical pen-and-ink drawings have illustrated more than 30 children's books. Hanson is also an accomplished weaver. A graduate of Carleton College, Hanson enjoys tennis, skiing, sailing, reading, traveling, and walking in the woods surrounding her home.

Make Me Laugh!

101 ANIMAL JOKES
101 FAMILY JOKES
101 KNOCK-KNOCK JOKES
101 MONSTER JOKES
101 SCHOOL JOKES
101 SPORTS JOKES
CAT'S OUT OF THE BAG!
DUMB CLUCKS!
ELEPHANTS NEVER FORGET!
FACE THE MUSIC!
GO HOG WILD!
GOING BUGGY!

GRIN AND BEAR IT!
IN THE DOGHOUSE!
LET'S CELEBRATE!
OUT TO LUNCH!
OUT TO PASTURE!
SNAKES ALIVE!
SOMETHING'S FISHY!
SPACE OUT!
STICK OUT YOUR TONGUE!
WHAT'S YOUR NAME?
WHAT'S YOUR NAME, AGAIN?